DevOps Adoption

A Must-Have For Any IT Leader Facing Digital Tranformation

By Christopher Weller

© **Copyright 2017 by Christopher Weller - All rights reserved.**

Respective authors own all copyrights not held by the publisher.

The following publication is reproduced below with the goal of providing information that is as accurate and reliable as possible. Regardless, purchasing this publication can be seen as consent to the fact that both the publisher and the author of this book are in no way experts on the topics discussed within and that any recommendations or suggestions for example those that made herein are for informational purposes only. Professionals should be consulted as needed prior to undertaking any of the action endorsed herein.

This declaration is deemed fair and valid by both the American Bar Association and the Committee of Publishers Association and is legally binding throughout the United States.

Furthermore, the transmission, duplication or reproduction of any of the following work including specific information will be considered an illegal act irrespective of if it is done electronically or in print. This extends to creating a secondary or tertiary copy of the work or a recorded copy and is only allowed with express written consent from the Publisher. All additional right reserved.

The information in the following pages is broadly considered to be a truthful and accurate account of facts and as such any inattention, use or misuse of the information in question by the reader will render any resulting actions solely under their purview. There are no scenarios in which the publisher or the original author of this work can be in any fashion deemed liable for any hardship or damages that may befall them after undertaking information described herein.

Additionally, the information in the following pages is intended only for informational purposes and should thus be thought of as universal. As befitting its nature, it is presented without assurance regarding its prolonged validity or interim quality. Trademarks particular are mentioned without written consent and can in no way be considered an endorsement from the trademark holder.

The trademarks particularly used are without any consent, and the publication of the trademark is without permission or backing by the trademark owner. All trademarks and brands within this book are for clarifying purposes only and are the owned by the owners themselves, not affiliated with this document.

Table of Contents

Introduction..1

    Understanding the Significance of DevOps 5

Chapter 1 Adopting DevOps at Enterprise Scale 9

    Integrating Applications and Reducing Risk.................. 11

    Steps to a Successful DevOps Adoption......................... 14

    Automation Approach... 25

Chapter 2 Overcoming DevOps Adoption Challenges 27

Chapter 3 Optimizing IT Operations with DevOps.......... 35

    Transformation to Optimization and Continuous Innovation 36

    Cost Savings with DevOps 40

    Maximizing Innovation 46

Chapter 4 Metrics for Measuring DevOps Success............51

Chapter 5 the Impact of DevOps on IT Organizations 57

    The Importance of Automation in Maximizing Efficiency.. 61

Conclusion... 68

Introduction

DevOps techniques and methods are breaking software operations and software development barriers, especially in recent time. DevOps has been greatly helpful when it comes to the software development since it provides more frequent releases, which ultimately provide to organizations and companies an edge on a certain time to market.

Companies and organizations are now able to release products more often as well as to push fixes to their customers in the span of just a few hours. DevOps is a movement which implements a collection of practices which automate the various processes between IT teams and software development team, so they can easily build as well as test software quicker and then release it with greater reliability.

The fundamental concept of DevOps is mainly founded on a concept of building a culture of greater collaboration between development and IT operations teams, which historically mainly functioned in the relative silos. There are many benefits of DevOps approach including faster software releases, increased trust, ability to solve some critical issues faster and greater ability to manage various unplanned work and tasks.

DevOps is the most famous next portmanteau, which greatly speaks of its popularity, especially in recent years. DevOps has emerged to be among the most popular software development concepts namely bringing together only the best of IT operations and software development. DevOps in its essence is a movement, a culture as well as a philosophy. We can also say that it is a type of a firm handshake between operations and development, which greatly emphasize a shift in better collaboration, mindset and tighter integration.

DevOps also unites continuous delivery, agile concept, automation and more in order to help operations and development team to be more innovative, more efficient as well as to be able to deliver higher value to their customers and businesses.

When it comes to the origin of DevOps movement, it all started to coalesce at the beginning of 2007. At the time, major software development and IT operations communities got more vocal about what they felt was a fatal level of increased dysfunction in the industry.

They mainly railed against some traditional software development model, who mainly called for those who are involved in writing a code to be more functionally and organizationally apart from others who are involved in deployment as well as the support of the code. IT professionals and developers had separate and commonly competing objectives.

They are commonly separated into some independent departments and they also have separate key performance indicators which served as a judge of their work. These teams commonly work on separate floors and even in separate buildings. That resulted in kind of separated teams that greatly concern only about their fields of expertise, botched releases, long hours and unhappy customers.

However, major software development and IT operation teams were certain that there is a better way. The two communities decided to get together and start talking with people like Gene Kim, Patrick Dubois and John Willis who were driving that conversation.

The talks began in some online forums as well as some local meet-ups. However, the topic today is among the major themes when it comes to the software development and IT operations.

The topic has brought many companies and organizations together, and major software development companies look forward to incorporating DevOps techniques into their businesses. Strictly speaking, people are not surprised since separated teams within a company or organization, in fact, form broken lines of communication as well as no proper collaboration. Collaboration and communication are greatly required or even mandatory especially in the IT industry.

Agile movement concept is used commonly for development and planning, but still, there is a great struggle in order to get the code without great drama. You have probably heard many great things about DevOps approach, and I have to be honest, most of them are true.

DevOps has brought great changes into the industry especially when it comes to the product management, IT operations, and IT security.

However, it should be noted that DevOps is not working like a magic, and certain transformations cannot happen just like that overnight. On the other hands, the good news is that you do not have to wait a long period of time for upper management to roll great products released very frequently.

It is important to understand a true value of DevOps approach that will most certainly bring small as incremental changes, and both you and your team can embark on this adventure right away.

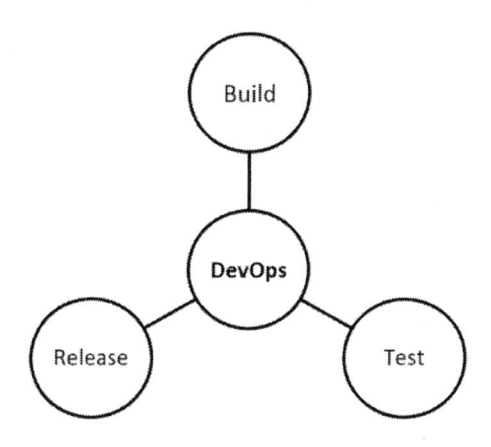

Understanding the Significance of DevOps

It is more than apparent that there is the rise of the DevOps movement and culture and there are many reasons why the approach has been accepted by many organizations and corporations in recent time. There are commonly present IT-enabled innovations as well as a competitive differentiator for all types as well as for all sizes of organizations. The ability to run software reliably and the ability to deliver IT systems more often are critical in the industry. This concept is one that gives the DevOps concept this great importance as well as rise.

DevOps mainly aims to break down great barriers and some conflicting priorities, which often exist between operations teams and development teams like application performance, project spend and functional requirements.

DevOps approach allows every team to work in a greater collaboration that results in delivering systems into production stage safely, reliably and rapidly. It also allows teams to support and operate the system effectively.

It should be noted that DevOps is a culture rather than a certain method of technology. It mainly aims to develop greatly collaborative working relationships as well as to foster adoption of a common collection of objectives in order to deliver IT services, which provide greater value to the various businesses.

DevOps is also associated with another set of methods and techniques Continuous Delivery. These methods are an amazing synthesis of concepts from continuous integration, lean production, and continuous deployment.

However, traditionally there has been a little working partnership between operations teams and development teams. On the other hand, DevOps approach has brought these teams together to work in harmony and deliver greater products more frequently. Culture is the number one success factor in the approach. Building DevOps culture of transparency, shared responsibility and faster feedback is the fundamental ground of every high-performing team, which uses DevOps approach.

DevOps approach also allows teams to release faster as well as to work smarter, and speed is everything in the industry. Teams that practice DevOps release with higher stability and quality. Lack of review cycles and automated tests, in fact, block the release to production as well as poor incident response times commonly kills velocity as well as team confidence.

On the other hand, teams are able to increase productivity as well as release more frequently with fewer issues and hiccups. DevOps approach also accelerates time to resolution since the team with faster feedback look is that team which thrives.

Seamless communication and full transparency enable teams in order to minimize downtime as well as to resolve issues faster. In the case when critical issues are not resolved fast, customer satisfaction greatly tanks.

DevOps approach also helps to manage unplanned work. An unplanned work is a reality that almost every team has to face. This reality influences overall team productivity. However, DevOps approach clears prioritization, so the teams are able to manage unplanned work while continuing to dedicate on the previously planned work.

Chapter 1 Adopting DevOps at Enterprise Scale

The speed of businesses today greatly affects every part of a company and organization with no exceptions. This is the main reason why traditional approaches and techniques of deploying and developing software tend to split the process into separate departments and methods are commonly being replaced by new as well as more agile techniques like as DevOps. DevOps approach is able to move silos in order to get processes, people and tools all working together in order to make product delivery and deployment faster as well as more predictive.

DevOps movement is greatly changing the overall IT environment and it incorporates into various areas including the database. It should be noted that some areas, like major areas affected by DevOps, have not been part of some traditional development models. There is a new research recently carried out which shows how great impact of DevOps is of the overall IT world. A global study, which included around thousand companies and organizations, surveyed IT professionals using SQL Server. These IT professionals are ranging from IT directors and managers to C-level executives and administrators. The study shows that half of them employed more than five hundred people. The message was clear. DevOps movement, in fact, is becoming a norm as well as mainstream. More and more people clearly see that the database is central to the software development process.

Recent studies have shown that more than eighty percent of people have already adopted DevOps methods. On the other hand, numerous people plan to adopt it over the course of the next three years. The bigger the company or organization, the more likely that it will move further and work on adopting DevOps in the near future. It should be noted that around fifty-nine organizations and companies with over thousand employees have already adopted and switched to DevOps practices and incorporated DevOps techniques into their business.

IT services, as well as retail, are potentially reflecting the overall competition in the market since they are leading their ways. Over fifty percent of companies and organizations are already using DevOps techniques like major healthcare and finance companies. DevOps also greatly affects manufacturing, government, education as well as large nonprofit organizations. Therefore, it is not surprising that you are thinking about adopting DevOps practices and incorporating them into your own business since major companies have already done that with great success.

Integrating Applications and Reducing Risk

Many major companies have already integrated DevOps into their business, but it should be noted that there are some obstacles on the path, which you should keep in mind. The greatest obstacle when it comes to the moving to DevOps environment commonly is a perceived lack of needed skills as well as a lack of alignment between operation teams and development teams. On the other hand, these obstacles are not something that you cannot overcome since those require just a little bit of effort in order to enhance greater collaboration between your teams. I believe that you are not in nine percent of people who are not planning on adopting DevOps methods.

Skills, in fact, are the greatest challenge on this journey. When it comes to the integrating different database changes into the process, it should be said that consistency is what matters. It is important to keep in mind that synchronizing database and application changes would be most probably the biggest challenge. Protecting business data would be an issue, but not if you properly incorporate DevOps into your organization or company. You will start with five fundamental steps, which follow DevOps adoption.

- Continuous Integration: Code changes will be merged with the mainline several times per day. The core of continuous integration are unit testing and TDD.

- Continuous Delivery: Code will be developed in short cycles and released more frequently

- Continuous Testing: Code will be continually tested in order to ensure quality before it is released.

- Continuous Feedback: The current state of the project needs to be determined.

- Continuous Monitoring: Shows real-time status of the application.

Companies are commonly integrating databases and applications in recent time. The old picture of those companies showed that they were made up of silos of database administrators and developers, which do not work collaboratively. However, this picture is far away from the truth. There were some companies and organizations, which have shown that they have great communication between their teams that meant that the teams were working together. However, DevOps approach has brought a better communication between the teams in order to provide greater efficiency and better products meaning release of the products is more frequent.

In major organizations, developers are responsible for building database scripts and product deployment and they work together with IT operations teams toward the same goal, reaching higher productivity and gain higher customer satisfaction.

When it comes to the major challenges, one notably involved in adopting, DevOps practices, it should be noted that risks are greatly reduced. For instance, in the traditional approach, there is a great risk of failed deployments as well as for downtime while making changes. This was mainly due to slow deployment cycles as well as due to inability to respond faster to various changing business requirements. Another issue regarding traditional approach is a poor visibility of various changes that greatly affect the overall management process. This clearly shows the fundamental importance of successful and fast database changes to every major business today.

For companies, which employ from five to ten thousand people, slow deployment cycles and slow development are a great drawback. The inability to respond quickly to various requirements that are ever-changing is deemed to be a downside. However, DevOps greatly reduces these risks moderately greater with traditional approach since deployment cycle times are faster. DevOps approach is providing ways in order to overcome these issues, so there is no wonder why it is rapidly gaining popularity.

The approach provides greater speed when it comes to the delivery as well as it adds greater value to the overall work of the companies and organizations. Development teams want to be able to focus on adding value work and they can do just that with DevOps. The approach also helps improving collaboration between the teams as well as it significantly reduces application downtime.

Steps to a Successful DevOps Adoption

It is more than apparent that adopting DevOps techniques and practices can greatly accelerate software releases, while at the same time it assures that application meets specified quality objectives. However, it should be noted that DevOps cannot be bolted on, bought or simply declared. Since you are considering moving away from traditional practices and adopt DevOps into your business, there are some steps, which you need to follow in order to incorporate it successfully.

It is important to find the most optimal way of implementing DevOps into your business. Your optimal way is one, which will enable greater agility as well as to rapid delivery of products and services to your customers. Your way also should be the one without compromising quality. Yes, I know these are the greatest challenges when it comes to this industry, but with DevOps, you are able to overcome all of them and provide the best possible service to your customers.

Many IT leaders have to agree that adopting DevOps techniques is significantly accelerating software releases and at the same time applications meet desired quality objectives. Therefore, there is no wonder why you want to move in toward the DevOps direction.

The first step on this journey is to warmly embrace a DevOps mindset in order to start. It should be noted that you could not start just by starting and starting using tools. It is important that your entire company and all teams have an understanding of what DevOps is and which needs it can address. Another important thing is that everyone within your company needs to be willing to these changes and to leave behind the ways thing have been done in the past.

In order to begin the process, you should identify application value streams by identifying series of all activities specifically necessary for moving your services and products from development to the production stage. In the process, you will see that there are various bottlenecks, constraints and of course, wait queues. However, by examining your applications value streams you will be able to understand on which activities your teams need to focus and what activities should and need to be improved.

As soon as you identify areas in which your delivery process is not so efficient, you will see what activities need to be improved since it is a great opportunity to make changes within your company or organization, which will most certainly provide better quality services and products. However, in order to achieve this, you have to accept changes and be willing to experiment. It should be noted that short-term failure is commonly accepted since you are learning from it as well as improving.

Therefore, do not let that to confuse you or discourage you. As long as you are learning, it is accepted. So, instead of accepting various not and so efficient ways of working, you have to encourage the entire organization and all teams to ask themselves important questions which can give you an answer like how to improve and make the process more efficient.

You may hear that companies and organizations equate DevOps approach with automation. Well, already stated is true strictly speaking since automation can easily help in order to accelerate various manual processes. On the other hand, DevOps is mainly about communication and collaboration. In other words, you have to embrace firm collaborative practices and communication among everyone including testing teams, software development teams, delivery teams and other.

One of the most important initiatives in DevOps approach is most certainly selecting the right metrics in order to record as well as to track process. You should keep in mind that establishing the right baseline of DevOps metrics is crucial.

You should keep that in mind to make the most of the metrics early in the process and you should not be afraid to measure things that initially might seem not that good. However, measuring metrics is the fundamental step, which will demonstrate your progress over time as well as it, will show you real business benefits to some senior leadership.

Most Useful DevOps Metrics:

- Mean-time to recover: It shows how long it would take applications in the production stage to recover from a failure.

- Mean time to production: It shows how long it would take when new code is committed into certain code repository for it to be deployed into the production stage.

- Average lead-time: It shows how long it would take for a new requirement to be tested, build, delivered and deployed into the production stage.

- Deployment speed: It shows how fast you can deploy some new version of applications to a certain environment like staging, integration, test, preproduction or production.

- Deployment frequency: It shows how often you can deploy new release candidates to staging, test, preproduction and production environments.

- Production failure rate: It shows how often the software fails during the production during a certain period of time.

It should be noted that there are many other metrics you can use, but you should try to avoid using metrics which look impressive, but don't tie to the overall business benefit. You should avoid metrics moderately easily gained since these will make your team look good, but they don't actually do nothing when it comes to the contributing to the overall business improvements.

As soon as you determine metrics, you will have to collect and have a baseline including information like where you currently stand, your goals regarding the each metric, so your team will know in which direction to move and what to strive for.

It should be noted that you have to constantly share business goals, progress, and metrics with everyone who is involved. You can set up metrics dashboard which will display current metrics as well as progress toward your goals. It is crucial that you provide a complete transparency for your team since it will greatly foster effective collaboration and communication and at the same time it will break down barriers between operations and development teams in the process.

You should apply Lean principles which accelerate feedback as well as improve time to value.

- Get idea into production fast
- Get your team to use it
- Get feedback

Continuously Improve:

- Application delivered
- Environment deployed
- Application and environment delivery process

The next step is to understand as well as to address your needs and business goals. It should be noted that in order to start, you should't just drop into some automated tool or hire a DevOps engineer and later expect success. The truth is that every company and organization have a unique DevOps journey and in their case it is tied to their specific culture and business, and their journey will be more about changing business habits as well as communications patterns. You will have your own unique journey as well and tools only work in order to enable automation, and DevOps is much more than just tools.

DevOps is an approach and way of accelerating the creation as well as delivery of quality software. However, it will succeed only if you and your team focus on what makes business sense for your company. You and your team should focus on improving the security, usability and other fundamental attributes your customers care about. You should balance efficiency and effectiveness in order to deliver the right thing in the right way. In order to do so, you will use a Lean and Agile concept since these concepts are the heart of DevOps approach.

> Lean Concept: Reduce work and eliminate bottlenecks and waste

> Agile Concept: Provides fast response times, small batch sizes and continuous feedback

The next step is to focus on adopting DevOps iteratively. When you start, you shouldn't try to boil the ocean with an immediate DevOps initiative. First, you should identify a pilot application from your cross-functional team which includes operations and development team. The next step is to examine your value stream in order to determine bottlenecks and constraints which will serve for further creation of an initial development pipeline which addresses your process constraints. You should also measure success, progress, rinse, repeat and wash.

Generally speaking, at the beginning you should look at tackling biggest value stream constraints since by doing so you will, in fact, have the largest impact on your business. It should be noted that some of the constraints are not easy to resolve and they might take a longer period of time in order to be corrected. On the other hand, there are constraints which you can easily resolve and they take almost no time in order to be corrected. However, this process may take longer than anticipated since you may need to convince others to change before doing anything of this.

You also want to go through iterations in order to build confidence in the process framework as well as the pilot before you expand to some other projects. It is important that you are sure in your process and its metrics before you move on other processes like applying lessons to another team.

The most important thing is to make sure that your teams are at the same time influence who are able to take these principles and adopt them. You know that keeping your expertise locked up is not helpful when it comes to the expanding practices to the enterprise successfully.

Since you are at the very beginning of your DevOps journey, you should consider starting from delivery process and later move toward production stage. It is important to properly implement branch management techniques. Building automation, in fact, is the key when it comes to the fast feedback which will enable an efficient downstream process in the future of your business.

Once you are done with building automation and comprehensive continuous integration, you are ready to move toward your goal faster and effectively. You will be able to begin shifting your activities as well as speed up delivery over time.

Fundamental Business Drivers:

- Driving business agility
- Scaling for the enterprise
- Driving innovations

The next step is to emphasize quality assurance earlier in the process. When it comes to the major companies and organizations, it is more than apparent that testers, in fact, get the least amount in order to do quality assurance. This eventually leads to product suffering in terms of its quality.

Companies and organizations which greatly struggle with DevOps methods often mainly focus their efforts on automating deployments, but at the same time, they are overlooking the needs when it comes to the quality assurance.

It should be noted that it is impossible to automate every step of your testing in DevOps, but on the other hand, it is critical to focus on automating all test which runs as part of your overall continuous integration process including static code analysis, unit tests and other. Regression testing and smoke testing are performed in every environment within a delivery process, so they are critical when it comes to the automating process.

Automating at least some of the functional testing as well as some nonfunctional tests is greatly associated with performance, security and other quality related features which can often be accomplished to speed up the overall process and all other activities. You should run long tests which commonly require production related environments late in your process. However, these tests would not slow down initial feedback cycles which must be quick.

Automation Approach

When it comes to the automation, you should take the smart approach since automation is the fundamental step toward accelerating delivery processes and accelerating everything else like configuration, infrastructure, build, test platform, overall process, etc. Automation should be defined as well as written in code.

When you embark on something particularly broken, time-intensive or prone to errors, logical step is to start automating in that environment first and then move to the other environments. This will benefit your team greatly by reducing delivery times, eliminating configuration drift and increasing repeatability. You should standardize your approach towards automation to ensue operations, development, quality assurance and every team in between to have a common frame and reference as well as common language in order to deliver tasks efficiently and more frequently.

Another important thing is to use software engineering techniques when you are building DevOps automation. Infrastructure is just like a code and it should be designed and implemented with some coding standards, namely effectively tested under certain configuration control. It will be further documented as well. When it comes to the quality of your automation process, it should be as important as the overall quality of your application. It should be noted that DevOps cannot be bolted on or simply declared.

DevOps practices are those, which help you, achieve success, but at the same time, it only can be achieved if you put there a lot of hard work as well as discipline. You have to be aware of the fact that it will take time and on this journey, there are some challenges as well which you can overcome with your hard work.

If you follow DeOps approach and its methods, you will be able to cover your bases and you will shortly see great influence of DevOps on your business. You have to remember that DevOps is a great journey, but a journey that never ends. There are always new ways in order to improve what you do and what your team does. However, if you never get started, you definitely will not reach your goals, so there is no better time to start than now.

Chapter 2 Overcoming DevOps Adoption Challenges

Many IT operation and software development teams have already adopted DevOps techniques into their work in order to gain help from it and to evolve into more innovative as well as a faster version of their former selves. Companies and organizations that have not yet implemented DevOps practices feel the great pressure to do so as a certain result of competition. The competition is widely present in the industry. However, pursuing advancement may be uncomfortable since it calls for all teams to move out of their work comfort zones. Progress also comes with many challenges at first, but it greatly pays off if you stay the course and put hard work and discipline.

One of the main challenges when it comes to the implementing DevOps practices is how to overcome the DevOps mentality. You already know that DevOps methods are all about integrating all teams together as well as breaking down those traditional silos, which exist within IT organizations and companies. There is also a consideration that developer team is tossing their code over some imaginary wall to the operations team. People also believe that developers try to innovate as well as to make changes quickly and operations teams try to maintain a hundred percent service levels. However, the truth is that the goals of both teams commonly counter each other when there are no DevOps practices involved.

Both teams have to work on aligning their goals and priorities in order to deliver more frequently and in higher quality. Handovers between the teams are commonly expensive which makes them a source of delay. Integrating various teams, in fact, is the heart of DevOps practice, it is the first hurdle, which any company, and organization needs to overcome on their journey of adopting DevOps practices.

Further, in the process of DevOps integration, some companies and organizations are moving toward cross functionality as well as product development teams that work collaboratively in order to manage their products. It should be noted that a broad cross functional team, in fact, align with products by owning its architecture, roadmap, design, run, development and support requirements. This, in fact, brings testers and other representatives of the business into the developer team and a great collaborative process. This may sound easy, but for major enterprises, it is very difficult to achieve since the process commonly involves breaking up some shared services, staff restructures and reporting lines. With this, there is often a political battle as well that org unit pays for, so org unit is the owner of the certain product.

Another DevOps challenge is how to move properly from legacy infrastructure to various micro-services. Older applications and infrastructure may be greatly problematic, even if those have served the organization or company for many years. Remaining on some legacy structure may spell huge stability problems as well as my lead to a lack of support, which will be left behind your advancing competition. Using infrastructure particularly a code related together with various micro-services is another huge step towards better future of continuous integration.

Infrastructure, in fact, modifies the overall development lifecycle in order to adapt ever-changing markets as well as to meet customer needs. In the case when company or organization does not stay innovative, it will be quickly replaced by some other company, which offers something better and more innovative to customers. Modifying or replacing older as well as monolithic application with a fewer number of micro-service architectures can often open up the floodgates to quicker innovation and faster development.

It should be noted that there might be a high barrier to entry with various micro-services. That entity has its own issues and problem, which need to be managed and resolved at some point. On the other hand, by moving to various micro-services from that legacy as well as monolithic infrastructure, you have to develop foundations of the automation process, continuous delivery, and configuration management all in one place in order to be able to cope with greatly increased operational workloads, which various micro-services bring.

You should keep in mind that too much focusing on tools is not that great idea. There is the exciting prospect when it comes to the adopting DevOps concept, and there are many new flashy tools as well. However, many organizations and companies believe that if they use multiple tools, they will reach their goals faster. Strictly speaking, it is not the case. It should be noted that with the introduction of these flashy tools, you have to pay attention to train your staff to use them properly as well as to ensure that your staff meets certain security requirements as well. It is also important to make sure that tools that your team uses are well-integrated with the already existing infrastructure. However, a tool may divert you greatly from your fundamental priority, your team.

Your org structure and your team are critical to any DevOps practice and once you have designed the correct structure, your team should follow it in collaboration.

As soon as you define your process, you are able to determine the tools, namely required to meet your process. Before doing so, make sure you and your teams are focused more on the process rather than on various tools. The most important factor when it comes to the transitioning to DevOps practices is your team. In other words, if your team is not trained in a proper manner, there will be a great confusion regarding newly implemented tools and processes. Another great challenge when it comes to the adopting DevOps is frequent resistance to change. The transition to DevOps may seem scary to your team and key stakeholders. However, explain it as a certain evolution of some current development practices rather than some kind of revolution, which can help with that issue. You should not be telling people to change since that may result in some bad reflection.

The change will come in some time, but it cannot happen overnight, it must be gradual and smooth. This, in fact, will allow everyone from your team to embrace DevOps practices and culture since they will slowly become accustomed to these changes and they will realize that these new ways can greatly contribute to the overall development process. It is better to find a full application or small product and remodel it into DevOps practices. Your team will see the benefits of those practices when they see them in action, so other teams will also want to adopt the changes. This will steadily ease that sense of unfamiliarity and it will get everyone on board ready to embark on DevOps journey.

There is also a challenge when it comes to the Dev and Ops clashes since those teams are having separate metrics and tool sets. It is greatly beneficial to sit both of your teams down and to seek to better understand where it really makes sense to adopt and integrated the tools they commonly use as well as to unify various metrics they often monitor. However, some teams may be not so willing to take part in the discussion, and they are unwilling to move away from legacy tools, simply put not just technologically inferior but as well slow down the infrastructure mainly due to various compatibility issues.

You should make sure that the tools, specifically being adopted, are greatly aligned with your goals and that they do not cause any distractions from your main objective and those are the applications, which will be developed. Overcoming these challenges will provide smoother DevOps transition at the very beginning. Over a period of time, team members will simply get used to these changes and the feeling of constant innovation. Innovation is crucial when it comes to this industry since the competition is huge.

Once your teams learn how to communicate on a higher level and how to cooperate, they will determine certain ways of helping each other. The discomfort of change, in fact, is better than staying behind your competition due to fear of changes and not being innovative.

You should not fear of failure and you should not constantly worry if DevOps in your case will be successful. DevOps in much more than just some technical practices and DevOps impacts people as well as processes, so as soon as you start keeping that in mind. You should draw a certain connection between overall management's goals and other goals, which can be improved by DevOps practices. You have to think about what pressures and goals managements is facing. A common goal is to increase overall operational efficiency and it is usually accomplished by some shorter task, times as well as lowering costs.

If you want to greatly influence senior management and your entire organization or company, you should phrase your proposal in a certain way, which speaks loudly to management's goals. In order to overcome DevOps adoption challenges, keep an eye the legacy systems, application complexity, testing automation, managing various environments, skillset, your budget, executive support, and tools.

Chapter 3 Optimizing IT Operations with DevOps

You are aware of the fact that there is a constant change in the IT world. Change continues to rise. The speed of innovation is also changing over the time. It is more than apparent that it is of crucial importance to keep pace in order to cope with the competition as well as to realize value for your company or business. DevOps techniques, in fact, provide a new approach, which makes keeping up with the competition more achievable. DevOps is a philosophy as well as a movement, which greatly can influence and accelerate time to value, increase business productivity and improve product quality across different organizations and companies in order to deliver more value, but in less time specifically crucial in this industry.

The advantages of DevOps approach ultimately are more than apparent across multiple organizational layers since the approach greatly encourages collaboration, communications, and integration between IT operations and software development team. The approach also helps IT sector to serve the overall business more effectively as well as it provides opportunities for the business to work seamlessly for employees and for its customers.

In order to meet the demand specifically present in the software development world, integrations, business offerings, and partnerships really must be fully embraced by your team in order to deliver the best from DevOps approach. When it comes to the rampant innovation, it is more than necessary in order to set certain standards of excellence instead just following some other standards. Crucial for achieving DevOps success is to have a highly automated system that can easily scale out with your overall business growth.

Driving business agility:

- Continuous delivery
- Shift left test
- Shift left Ops engagement
- Lean application delivery

Transformation to Optimization and Continuous Innovation

Businesses always have to search for new ways in order to transform to find more efficient and better ways to deliver their value faster to their customers or users. Some of the motivating factors are streamlined value flow, shorter lead times and reduction of their costs and bound capital, namely requiring enterprises to move towards a transition to optimization model and continuous innovation.

The most prominent examples may be found when you study the last decade in various industries like the automobile industry. You will see that companies involved in a specific industry have their ways of automating and optimizing their end-to-end production process. DevOps approach as well as delivery, continuous integration and deployment all, in fact, draw the analogies to the overall manufacturing world as well as explain how software industry can greatly benefit from DevOps practices.

When it comes to the high performers in the industry, they have two hundred times more frequent deployments, three times lower change failure rate, twenty-four times faster mean to recovery and two thousand times faster lead time than their peers, it is not surprising that you want to move towards DevOps practices.

Many industries have transformed significantly especially in recent years, and those changes have an impact on the software industry as well. This digital transformation has been already experienced by many organizations and companies since it boils down to greatly faster lead times and even more important it will commonly lead to optimizing the value process as well as to continuous integration for your end-users.

You are aware of the fact that traditional waterfall model with Lead Time has taken several weeks or even months to be completed. This is a certain reality check, which clearly shows that it is the right time to move to this new approach and left behind traditional models and approaches. Continuous optimization and continuous innovation have a Lead Time namely measured in minutes compared to waterfall measurements that have taken several weeks.

Continuous optimization and continuous integration provide immediate customer feedback since you optimize before you deploy. Delivering value through different software, in fact, has become instant and the closed feedback loop is back to engineering in short time, which greatly saves your time and reduces overall process cost as well as risk.

Continuous delivery provides an early feedback expressly entirely automated. Your team will be able to test some new features internally and externally through various early access programs as well as different testing. That will provide you an early feedback and at the same time, your team will be working on other features. This greatly prevents delayed or late feedbacks that commonly occur using other traditional models and approaches.

You should build trust through automated feedback loops. When it comes to the biggest challenges you may encounter, the adoption of a continuous deployment model requires a great trust between your teams. This is the greatest challenge, which you have to overcome through automated feedback loops. As soon as you build trust in everyone working in your company or organization, you will be able to push your code through the delivery pipeline successfully and all the way into the hand of your customers.

It should be noted that trust has to be earned, and in the transition phase the trust must be accepted in the way, that there will be challenges, but those challenges can be resolved. You should remember that failure is not something that deserves punishment. However, every failure should lead to learning and improvement, so future delivery processes will pass beyond failure.

DevOps is more a cultural change and mindset rather than some new technology. It mainly streamlines in order to provide greater collaboration and communication between teams within a single organization or company. DevOps can greatly improve your goals as well as deliver products that increase your business value at the same time reducing your overall business cost and risks. The collaboration can greatly improve overall efficiency, optimize the entire software cycle, reduces costs, pay ways towards innovations as well as to render a competitive edge.

It should be noted that DevOps is a great challenge and just like any other challenge it also contains a collection of certain loopholes which can prove to be the roadblocks when it comes to the leveraging the full potential of the DevOps implementation. There are many ways to overcome DevOps adoption challenges discussed previously in the book. However, the direct overcome of implemented automation is higher efficiency which actively adds on to the greater savings in your business. Therefore, automation and DevOps must work in collaboration. Automation of various tasks reduces multiple manual operations, which lead to improving the speed of overall software development and software release.

Cost Savings with DevOps

When it comes to the certain ways on how DevOps can help you save your cost, there are many ways to incorporate

DevOps, which will lead to reduced overall costs. Automation, in fact, allows carrying various repetitive tasks such as performance testing and regression quickly even for some minor changes that are often time to consume. However, since DevOps practices provide repeatability, a cost is reduced at the very beginning. It, in fact, can bring down some manual efforts like running in several hours to greatly shorter runs that can be executed without any human supervision.

You are able to fashion multiple-deployment or single-build model with automation that can greatly reduce that time needed per each release as well as reduce manual stuff to release by some huge margins. It should be noted that automation leads to various improvements like reducing release time up to eighty-nine percent as well as reducing human resource dependencies by seventy-five percent.

Unplanned application downtime commonly costs a fortune, which means billions for major organizations and companies. Infrastructure failure causes a huge loss that also measures in fortune for large enterprises. It is fair to say that today downtime costs easily can be the death-knell of the overall business and customers and consumers, in fact, do not have the patience with those failed services. Service continuity and business integration are essential in order to stay in the race and to cope with the competition. Therefore, automated processes like fast rollovers and frequent backups using cloud- based technology greatly help in order to create a robust and stable system that further greatly reduced costs caused by failed services and downtime.

DevOps mainly promotes great cohesion, which should exist between all business stakeholders including developers, business heads, IT management and operations staff. Automatic update in real-time or tracking dashboard and reports as well as an automated set of metrics are used in order to gauge process in different stages regarding the software cycle which further leads to increased transparency and visibility. It also attempts to break down huge silos that result from traditional hierarchical structures of companies and organizations.

It also inculcates a spirit of great mutual understanding where all team members are aware of the issues regarding development side and all other areas involved in the software development. This also promotes proactive collaboration and communication as well as a greater sense of ownership where every member in the software chain gets that sense of belongingness especially aligned to the mutual business goal. A collaborative team, in fact, has greater chances of faster delivery specifically reducing chances of some cost overruns, which mainly occur due to schedule as well as due to expectations mismanagement.

DevOps approach also provides automated monitoring as a breeding ground for all new ways of improving your overall business process. It, in fact, enables you to identify as well as to mitigate risks at the stage where they are still controllable. When you mitigate and foresee risks, you are able to take better and wiser business decisions. It should be noted that each major risk not handled or avoided in some timely manner means saving additional operational costs that have occurred due to various interrupted operations. When it comes to the major DevOps advantages, I have to mention the timely discovery of defects and early testing. These allow team members to start testing in the early stage of software development to find defects as well as to fix them at the time when the cost of those fixes is very low. Automated testing allows that continuous testing to be a greater part of the DevOps practices like there is a direct feedback system scilicet able to catch the faults as well as to encourage innovations for further process improvements. This, in fact, brings down your overall cost.

There are many key objectives of DevOps approach like encouraging continuous delivery at the stage where small updates and changes can be easily developed, deployed and tested with greater speed. In the process automation rapidly becomes inherent in the overall process in order to support continuous delivery as well as continuous integration. This, in fact, helps to lay a better foundation and to have a stronger infrastructure as well as to create a robust application for customers and at the same time, you are avoiding great operational delay costs.

DevOps approach improves your business from multiple directions. Automation is able to help to business bring down time and cost and to improve quality as well as to promote scalability. It also is able to facilitate efficiency, predictability, and consistency that directly impacts the bottom line of your business and instills confidence in your team. Regulatory and audit bodies are able to get compliance metrics via automation, that can be of great importance when it comes to the getting quality accreditations in a smoother manner which greatly enhances your market creditability.

DevOps Adoption Model			
	Inefficient	Leaner	Leaner and Smarter
Steer	Process-based	Product-based	Optimizing
Develop and Test	Process-heavy	Agile	More Predictable
Deploy	Manual	Automated	More Transparent
Operate	Siloed	Collaborative	More Continuous

- Steer and measure the product in order to get an honest insight into value and progress

- Accelerate development times as well as test feedback cycles through various agile methods in order to reduce uncertainties

- Automate the release process and build in order to enable frictionless deployment

- Collaborate consistently across the entire software supply chain in order to get holistic efficiencies

- Optimize decisions with better continuous feedback, steering and analytics

- Increase the predictability of development through agile proficiency and leaner methods

- Improve the overall transparency of deployment updates through automation

- Improve the continuity of operations with fewer defects and better quality

Maximizing Innovation

Innovation is increasingly cited as the greatest competitive advantage when it comes to the business meeting its various digital challenges. However, innovations and their importance are commonly widely misunderstood and mistakenly reduced to some sophisticated features in the IT world. Innovation is much more as a competitive matter since it is primarily the overall process of translating various ideas or inventions into some high-value technology features that add greater value services to the overall business. In order to be called an innovation, a service or technology need to create a new value to its customers and consumers that would satisfy customers' needs and wishes. DevOps is commonly seen as the perfect way to make your organization or company an innovative champion. However, there are many consultants and solution vendors who have failed to bring innovations and achieve this goal due to oversimplifying the overall process. It should be noted that DevOps is a part of the process, not the process itself so it is not the end, but just the means. You should define your strategy with the innovation virtuous circle that can make your organization or company coping better with the competition. However, it is as a simplistic as some other investing sophisticated technologies. It all starts with defining your certain strategy and further continues with implementing your strategy throughout your entire IT business's value stream. It ends up with getting it implemented across your overall business. Organizational transformation and improvisation are not those good friends. You should rely on some proven frameworks, which can safely guide your effort step by step. In fact, it is the purpose of innovation virtuous circle that greatly facilitates as well as accelerates your overall innovations strategy and your efforts.

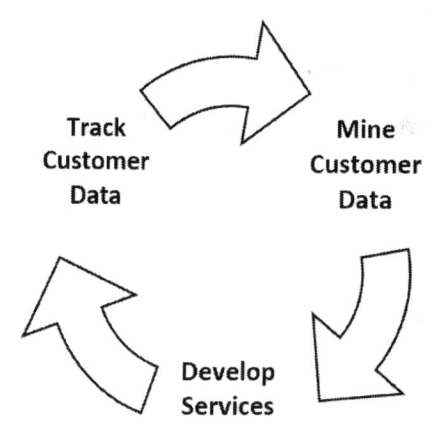

Track Customer Data → **Mine Customer Data** → **Develop Services** → (cycle)

The concept that lay underneath the innovation virtual cycle is the notion. It is keeping your customers loyal through some innovation guarantees revenue. The main idea is that the more innovation you provide, the more revenue and more loyal customers you will have. You should put together IT stakeholders and your business teams in order to discuss how to keep your customers loyal that will eventually ensure that you have continuous revenue. You should clarify the agile practices, processes, tools, partners, and skills by which your customer data will be obtained as well as tracked for further analytics purposes. The following step is to identify certain agile practices and processes, skills, partners and tools, which will help you in order to spot some innovative solutions, ideas, and technologies.

You should clarify the agile processes in order to ensure high quality, high frequency, and speedy innovation delivery. The last step is to identify the agile practices and processes, tools, partners and skills that will help you to monitor overall customer satisfaction as well as to improve overall customer experience. What you get when you follow these steps is a greatly comprehensive strategy which includes your goals of keeping your customers loyal and raising your estimated revenue.

DevOps can help you to reconfigure your overall IT value stream. Once you define your strategy, the following step is to use your value stream framework in order to deploy it throughout your IT business. The value stream, in fact, represents value interactions, skills, processes, practices and tools notably mobilized within your company or organizations in order to deliver innovation. The agile IT value stream conceptually is able to structure the IT value stream into multiple stages processes. Each stage, in fact, is widely associated with your ultimate goal and it mobilizes certain elements of your specific innovation strategy. You should focus on plan and measure, develop and test, release and deploy and monitor and improve. For planning and measuring, you should discuss your future business structure, roles and overall agenda with the infrastructure and tools that will be supporting analytics related innovations that will clearly show prioritization and your overall management portfolio. Plan and measure stage will gather your business priorities, solution vendors and strategy for continuous integration.

When it comes to the developing and testing stage, you should get a consensus on your staff in order to assign certain agile methodology together with continuous integration and testing which will greatly support your overall innovation development process. Develop and test stage will show you overall customer experience and overall customer value. Releasing and deploying stage involves discussing with your staff in order to assign as well as to release management and launch process together with the continuous deploy infrastructure particularly needed in order to support the overall process. Release and deploy stage will show you overall market responsiveness as well as continuous revenue.

Monitor and improve stage requirements discussing with your team in order to assign your products and services continuous improving together with various analytics technologies especially needed to support the overall process. Monitor and improve stage will show you customer value and customer experience. You will get documented and comprehensive blueprint of your business's value stream specifically transformed to DevOps. You will use it as a certain baseline in order to hire the solution vendor and consulting firms, which will configure your IT model to further innovations. Using the concepts of the innovative virtual cycle, you will establish your IT operational models, which will boost innovation. This transformation approach is used in order to provide greater innovation and to be able to cope with the competition. This approach greatly contributes and impacts your organization and provides a better insight into fundamental business analogies.

Chapter 4 Metrics for Measuring DevOps Success

We are aiming to do various things cheaper, quicker and with few bumps as possible. We have seen that DevOps can greatly reduce your cost; provide security as well as compliance acceleration, save testing and development cost, save monitoring cost and much more.

Your DevOps based service will instantly deliver when requested, it will be highly available and resiliency and it will have an elastic capacity. You will start by building support and momentum. You will establish new roles and pilot your new service design model and you will think of your service as life cycle since traditional IT is entirely project-based.

Infrastructure is built in response to certain application projects. In a service life cycle-based project, your infrastructure service will be designed and built outside of that context of a certain application project. As soon as you create infrastructure service, it will be available to your customers. The service will meet their needs. However, the initial creation of your infrastructure is not entirely tied to the business justification of that specific application project.

It should be noted that IT presents a service lifecycle, but it is not going deeper regarding some specific areas in every stage of that cycle. It mainly focuses on the service management processes regarding the every stage. Your company or organization will have to develop a certain methodology, which will define the certain activities specifically present in your service lifecycle.

When it comes to the metrics for measuring your DevOps success, these metrics can greatly help you in order to achieve your goals during your improvement project. Your team and you are taking that plunge into improved practices, and on your journey, metrics are, in fact, your best friend. Organizations make changes to their certain application lifecycle management tools, but they are not starting to measure what their performance at the moment is and how that changes, in fact, affect the overall performance. It is crucial to make the commitment to measurements and to monitor your performance on regular basis.

Since you have decided to improve your practices and process, you most likely have encountered on some issues including missed deadlines, long waits for small fixes and changes or on changes that cost too much. Issues include projects not getting fast to the production stage and projects that are running much longer than anticipated.

The quality of server configurations also may be an issue is the site is always down. Other great issues are long waits for small fixes and changes as well as changes, which cost too much to be executed and resolved on time. Another issue is if you have unsatisfied customers due to applications that are not working as customers expected.

If you have encountered some of these issues, then you are a perfect candidate for improving your overall process. It should be noted that before making any changes, first, you have to determine the issue areas for your certain organization and further, to begin with measuring your business capabilities as well as your team skills. Without a baseline, you will not be able to report effectively on your desired improvements.

The best way in order to improve your overall business is to obtain a wide range of metrics that will enable you to track your overall progress. There are many metrics, which you can choose like mean time to repair or recovery, a percentage of successful deployments, projects completed per quarter, percentage of successful deployments and many others.

In the following section, we are going to get a better insight into these metrics that most certainly will provide you a greatly balanced appraisal or your business capacity in order to provide operational fixes, capacity to deploy faster to production, develop new features as well as the ability to provide a greater return on your investment to business.

- Mean time to repair and recover: These metric measures how long it would take from when some incident is reported to that time when it is resolved. This number should be trending downwards. This also indicates both the capability of your team in order to deploy and resolve solutions as well as the responsiveness. You should be weighing your data in this metric by certain severity in order to avoid low-priority and low-severity issues from greatly skewing data. It should be noted that these kinds of issues are those that, in fact, are rarely resolved and you have to just filter out anything particularly things whichever are not considered as a high priority issue or incident. Your teams which will be optimized to use this metric, will ensure various things like that there is a rapid and short path through all available environments in order to get a fix through testing stage and into the production stage.

- Lead time: While this previous metric will greatly help you in order to monitor your team's ability to react to various customer support issues, the lead time will enable you to measure that exact time needed from the very beginning of development through deployment process to production stage. You want this metric to be as low as possible in order to highlight your team's ability. Your teams, which will be optimized for this metric, will mainly attempt to tackle smaller chunks of their work as well as to optimize the overall integration within the testing staff in order to shorten overall time you will need need for deployment process to be finished.

- Percentage of successful deployments: There are some organizations, which track their deployments as a percentage of some failed deployments, and they further try to greatly reduce the number of failures. However, the ultimate goal is to make sure that regardless of your deployment times, what is deployed doesn't cause any failures. A successful deployment is all about maintaining positive reactions and it is not about avoiding a certain outage when it comes to your customer base. A team, which will be optimized for these tasks, will tend to push some smaller as well as less risky changes more frequently.

- Projects completed per quarter: When it comes to the projects completed per quarter, increasing the number of total projects completed as well as launched to the production stage per quarter enables a faster return on your investment which you have turned into a certain project. This metric is great especially when it comes to the reporting success to your management as well as reporting success on your team's ability to execute. This is also used in order to provide confidence, which an investment in your team will generate, future results. This metric, in fact, leads your team to try harder to optimize for some smaller batches in order to get more projects done in a greatly reduced amount of time. Teams, which will be optimized for this metric, will also optimize towards delivery processes which support numerous projects all at once in order to avoid traditional project queue throughout the testing stage.

Chapter 5 the Impact of DevOps on IT Organizations

DevOps is both skillsets as well as a culture. We may also refer to DevOps as a philosophy. DevOps fundamentally aims to break down huge differences between operations and development teams in order to get everyone on the team working in collaboration towards the same direction. Major organizations and companies have been using IT internally since it is a part of their product development and their product portfolio. Department function and department heads have been greatly grappling with multiple simplifying processes. We know that the more complex things are the more of technology layers will be needed in order to make those things less complicated. In fact, it is managing those complicated things as well as other simplified processes.

The more you try harder to ensure that everyone on your team knows what other team members are doing, it seems like huge silos are created unwittingly. Functional departments and functional really start being encumbered by platforms as well as their own IT solutions and dashboard that they watch carefully with an eagle eye. IT platforms, silos, dashboards and solutions that are not compatible with each other, in fact, cannot be implemented with some existing systems.

It may be hard to believe, but this scenario is very common and still exists in various mid-sized as well as in large companies and organizations today. It should be noted that this certain scenario bleeds the organization of productive hours, its financial resources as well as go-to-market multiple delays where team's efficiency greatly suffers, and of course eventually, affects overall profitability.

The end game is to provide your operations and development team tools in order to act towards the same goal which will eventually lead to delivering higher quality and better software released more frequently. It is much like big data since it requires great cultural changes as well as breaking down silos that exist within your organization or company.

DevOps Benefits		
Less Effort	More Control	Greater Speed
Reduction in set-up time by up to 87 %	Single-click provisioning	67% acceleration in release cycle time
Reduction in environment downtime by up to 78 %	Faster adoption of best of breed tools and technologies	50% improved changes request throughput
Zero environment defects	Zero downtime for IT maintenance	30% reduction in development effort

In this industry, speed is everything and organization can no longer ignore various solutions, which can bridge both operations and development in measures, which make implementation of DevOps a great part of your as well as their overall IT, strategy. When it comes to the process businesses, you have to remember that DevOps is much more than a collection of tools. DevOps provides greater communication and collaboration within teams by utilizing continuous delivery and continuous integration methodology.

Software development takes time and software products take time as well. It also requires a lot of your effort as well as the effort of your team in order to ensure which versions are stable and functional in order to perform in the way it is supposed to be performed. Organizations and companies spend months of careful planning on preparatory work and on the process flow, the financials, the marketing and more, before the product is deployed. Organizations, in fact, have to contend with great walls between Dev and Ops which need to present a sense of interpersonal harmony, communications, and understanding what every function does. That further leads to a successful product launch.

It should be noted that increased complexity in terms of service offering, in fact, leads to visibility defects. Therefore, DevOps greatly influenced IT the world in terms of simplifying this web of various complexity via technology. There has been a great divide between development and operations teams, which only is amplified by notions that every group has their own goals. However, without a firm bridge between the teams, which addresses these various misconceptions of every team, business only, can face delays, obstacles, cost overruns and sometimes even irrecoverable failure. On the other hand, DevOps has brought these teams together to work in harmony towards the same goals.

Miscommunication and mismanagement really lead towards a dangerous road, which eventually affects the overall health of the business. However, DevOps practices reduce failure, reduce cost as well as improve overall business success as well as overall health of a business. Organizations and companies have to provide an integrated system which will feed into the different automation process and which will look at it completely holistically. That system will also build predictability around product workflow. In fact, DevOps practices have become an imperative, which cannot be ignored in order to maintain productive software development environment.

The Importance of Automation in Maximizing Efficiency

Organizations and companies undertake automation in order to cope and bring better efficiency when it comes to the management of their business. Running a business in this new-age economy, and not paying attention to faster time to deliver services and products to your customers is a huge mistake regardless of your line of business. DevOps encourages automation, so with DevOps practices organizations and companies are able to cope with their competition on a higher level. Bad practices lead to creating complications, which greatly affect development lifecycle. However, automating provides a better way in order to avoid complications and issues and when they happen, automating provides faster response and faster resolution to various issues. In order to achieve business success, both development and operations teams have to focus on improving overall performance by putting automation tool on the table which will most certainly improve quality, productivity, and measurability.

You should choose a reliable automation tool which can be easily implemented with already existing platforms like Microsoft, GitHub, AWS, Puppet, Selenium, New Relic, Jenkins, Chef, Sense and other. Organizations, which have adopted DevOps automation, in fact, have strong as well as a great positive impact on the industry. Adopting right DevOps practices helps organizations and companies to move towards better productivity and greater efficiency. Continuous delivery practices and lean management, in fact, have greatly contributed to stability and throughput. If you use right automation tools you can benefit from reduced cycles, higher quality of output, faster feedback loops and lower your overall costs of development. DevOps automation, in fact, leads to better quality of code, more frequent deploys and better testing. It also creates a certain culture of continuous improvement. IT organizations which have already adopted DevOps practices have thirty times more frequently deploys with two hundred times shorter lead times. These organizations also have sixty times fewer failures and they recover hundred sixty-eight times faster.

Major organizations like Facebook, IBM, and Etsy have already adopted DevOps practices. Etsy was able to improve a typical web development that took over an hour down to two minutes by using DevOps practices. On the other hand, Facebook was able to automate application deployments and operation system to 17,000 homogeneous and 17,000 heterogeneous servers just with a single Chef server. IBM also accelerated their capabilities in term of delivery by 400% in only eight months.

It is more than apparent that DevOps automation is the right way to go if companies and organizations need to greatly impress their customers, further remain competitive and of course thrive in this extremely volatile market. This is the place where delivery cycles time have greatly shrunk to weeks from several months and performance and stability of the product or application are fundamental metrics of business success. DevOps, in fact, is redefining this new organizational structure in terms of recognizing that new technology and improvements are needed in order to create an indelible impact as well as to enable greater productivity and efficiency of businesses. Organizations and companies have had their process as well as systems in order to monitor, test, track and deploy their products and services. There have been teams in those places too, who have worked hard, but within separated groups which made them operate in a manner, which was greatly debilitating. Today, the situation is different since there are many DevOps practices to be adopted and implemented into the businesses. DevOps, in fact, provides the maximum level of efficiency since it has introduced various automation tools, which have already built in visual dashboards that allow you to see all defects as well as bottlenecks that further help you to manage teams in a more effective manner by increasing stability, quality, throughput, and performance.

An automated tool can help you with continuous integration and continuous delivery including testing, version control of various IT artifacts, automated deployment, improve your productivity and well as improve overall profitability. It should be noted that regardless of your system, high-performance is achievable if your application is architecture for deployability and testability. You should not think that you are not able to implement DevOps into your system if your application runs on the certain mainframe. You should focus on the type of your system, but you should focus on re-architecting your system to be ready for deployability and testability.

Since there is a huge rise in adopting DevOps practices, major organizations and companies are seeking to hire a great number of professionals with major DevOps expertise. DevOps, in fact, is rapidly becoming a greatly valued skill for almost every It professional. It is not surprising since traditional Ops is great time consuming and it also requires more time in order to put out fires. On the other hand, organizations and companies which have already adopted DevOps practices spend more time on various infrastructure improvements, rather than on fixing issues and resolving complications.

Deployment Automation:

- Manage application versions and components
- Manage configuration acroos all environments
- Increase transparency
- Ensure compliancy and governance
- Offer secure self- service capabilities

Organizations and companies also are looking at various ways for resourcing their IT functions with highly skillful expertise. They are also redefining their ways in which Ops and Dev have operated. The world of DevOps automation is greatly fluid so it is moving in a specific direction. Major organizations and companies that have been using DevOps practices mainly see great organizational performance benefits. Firms whose methodology are DevOps practices also gain significantly in terms of productivity in comparison to those firms whose approach is not the DevOps.

The longer a company uses DevOps practices the higher their departments perform. It should be noted that high performing IT companies and organizations, in fact, have 50% lower failure rates than those medium and low performing IT companies and organizations. The potential of DevOps is huge so it is expected that more and more companies will soon adopt DevOps. It is also expected that open source tools will soon evolve in order to meet enterprise requirements.

The automation of DevOps is crucial for organizations to move in a direction towards success. More and more companies and organization have decided to move towards the path of DevOps adoption. This is not surprising if you look at various DevOps benefits. The way of doing various business is changing. Therefore, the way of managing IT operations and IT development have to change as well, and adopting DevOps is the right way to go and start making fundamental changes.

DevOps automation tools are definitely the right direction since it is more than apparent that today is the right time to break the silos as well as to harmonize your output for s common goal. The organizations and companies have to take that initiative and invest in DevOps practices since these are the key to improved business growth, success, effectiveness, productivity and overall business performance.

Conclusion

Since you are considering for transforming your IT environment, you want to achieve streamlined as well as rapid production by implementing DevOps practices into your business. DevOps is a perfect way when it comes to the enterprise, so there is no wonder why every major organization and company have already adopted DevOps methodology. Enterprises have their unique limitations, needs, capabilities as well as various challenges that all can be resolved with DevOps automation tools. In fact, DevOps has revolutionized enterprise IT.

DevOps provides high-value applications with greater velocity as well as agility. As soon as you adopt it, you will see the difference. By implementing DevOps practices, organizational and cultural changes and automation tools, you will head towards innovative and rapid experimentations. When it comes to this industry, speed is everything. Speed, in fact, is the greatest advantage when you face your competition. However, you should keep in mind that speed must never come at the expense of your product quality.

DevOps practices will allow your company or organization to keep operations at a high level, intersecting development and of course, quality assurance. When it comes to the enterprise-level DevOps practices, you will see that there are many challenges that you have to overcome. However, by implementing right DevOps automation tools, those challenges will not be an obstacle towards your business success. Your organization can keep low costs, low risks, as well as quality under control and at the same time, stay ahead of the competition as soon as you adopt DevOps practices into your business.

You will be able to adopt DevOps in large-scale various IT environments as well as to exceed traditional business goals and reach higher product release in more efficient and secure way. You will also achieve high-value optimization and innovation with low risk and cost. It is the right time to get your organization on board and innovate your way to the top. You can slip your production into the faster lane. There is no better time than now to embark on this journey.

Made in the USA
Lexington, KY
27 September 2017